Incredible
Fish

John Townsend

Raintree

Chicago, Illinois

For information, address the publisher:
Raintree, 100 N. LaSalle, Suite 1200, Chicago, IL 60602
Printed and bound in China
09 08 07 06 05
10 9 8 7 6 5 4 3 2 1

Library of Congress Cataloging-in-Publication Data
Townsend, John, 1955-
  Incredible fish / John Townsend.
     p. cm. -- (Incredible creatures)
Summary: Looks at the behavior and characteristics of different kinds of
fish, from the grazers that eat plants on the ocean floor to the
anglerfish, which has its own rod and line to catch other fish.
Includes bibliographical references and index.
  ISBN 1-4109-0529-2 (lib. bdg.) -- ISBN 1-4109-0853-4 (pbk.)
  1. Fishes--Juvenile literature. [1. Fishes.] I. Title. II. Series:
Townsend, John, 1955- Incredible creatures.
  QL617.2.T69 2005
  597--dc22
                              2003015747

Acknowledgments
The publishers would like to thank the following for permission to reproduce photographs: pp. 4–5, 9 (left), 10–11, 11, 12–13, 13, 14, 16–17, 19 (bottom), 19 (top), 20, 22–23, 24, 25, 26 (top), 34, 35, 36, 43, 45 (top), 48–49, 50, 50–51, 52 FLPA; pp. 4, 5 (top), 5 (middle), 5 (bottom), 6 (bottom), 7, 8, 9 (right), 10, 12, 15 (bottom), 15 (top), 16, 20–21, 22, 26 (bottom), 27, 28 (bottom), 29, 30–31, 33, 34–35, 37 (top), 37 (bottom), 38 (left), 38–39, 39 (right), 40, 40–41 Bill Wood/NHPA; p. 6 (top) Robert Yin/Corbis; p. 17 Tim Wright/Corbis; pp. 18, 24–25, 32 (left), 32–33 Oxford Scientific Films; p. 21 www.jphoto.dk; p. 23 Alexis Rosenfeld/Science Photo Library; p. 28 (top) John Downer/Nature Photo Library; p. 30 Ardea; p. 31 Nature Photo Library; p. 41 Image Quest 3-D; pp. 42, 42–43, 44, 45 (bottom), 46–47, 47, 49 NHPA; p. 46 Jacques Descloitres, MODIS Rapid Response Team, GSFC/NASA; p. 48 Jeffrey L. Rotman/Corbis; p. 51 Photofusion.
Cover photograph of a great white shark reproduced with permission of Getty Images (Image Bank)

The publishers would like to thank Mark Rosenthal and Jon Pearce for their assistance in the preparation of this book.

Contents

Some words are shown in **bold.** You can find out what they mean by looking in the glossary. You can also look out for them in the "Wild Words" bank at the bottom of each page.

Fantastic Fish!

Fast and old

- Tuna, swordfish, and some sharks are among the fastest fish. Some can reach 50 mi (80 km) per hour in short bursts.

- Sturgeon fish can live for more than 50 years, but we still do not know if other fish can live longer.

What is a fish? This may seem like a simple question, but the answer is not quite so easy. Do all fish live in water, have shiny scales, and fins? Some do, some do not.

There are three main types of fish. They live in either fresh water or salty seawater all around the world. Only a few **species** can live in both sorts of water.

The three types of fish are:
1. Bony fish. This is the biggest group, with about 20,000 species. That is 95 percent of all fish.
2. Bendable fish. There are about 1,000 species of these—with softer skeletons that are **cartilaginous.**
3. Jawless fish. These are **parasites** with mouths that suck on other fish.

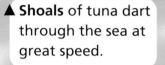

▲ **Shoals** of tuna dart through the sea at great speed.

cartilaginous   having soft, bendable gristle (cartilage) rather than bone
parasite   animal or plant that lives in or on another living thing

Bony fish

Fish were the first **vertebrates** to exist on Earth. Bony fish have skeletons made of bone. They come in many shapes and sizes. They usually have their mouths at the very front of their heads. These fish are found in freshwater rivers and lakes or in salty oceans. Very few fish can move from one type of water to the other, since the two **environments** are very different.

Bendable fish

Bendable fish have much softer skeletons. They are made of cartilage, the same material that makes the shape of your nose. Many of these fish, including rays and sharks, have their mouths on their undersides. Nearly all of these fish live in the sea.

Jawless fish

Jawless fish, such as hagfish, make the third group. They do not have actual fins and tails. Lampreys are jawless fish that live in the sea and in freshwater.

Find out later . . .

What was the great fish discovery of the 20th century?

What was the monster of Crofton Pond?

What is the most shocking fish?

▲ The great white shark can open its jaws to 3.3 ft (1 m) wide!

species type of living animal or plant
vertebrate any animal that has a skeleton with a backbone

Meet the Family

Did you know . . . ?

- The dwarf goby is the smallest fish. It is only 0.4 in. (1 cm) long.

All fish are different, but many are similar in some ways. So what do most fish have in common?

Fishy features

- Many fish have fins to **propel** them forward and for steering.
- Fish are usually smooth and **streamlined** (torpedo-shaped) to help them slip through the water. Fish are slippery, which helps them to move smoothly through the water without **friction.**
- Nearly all fish have slimy scales to keep their bodies waterproof. Scales come in different types and shapes, but they are like little plates of armor that overlap to protect the fish.
- Fish have tiny **sensors** along their heads and sides. These sensors detect pressure changes in the water when other animals come near.

▲ Goby fish come in many sizes and colors.

▲ The sea bass is a typical streamlined shape and covered in scales.

camouflage   color or pattern that matches the background
friction   drag or force when things rub together

- Fish come in all colors and patterns. Some have very good **camouflage,** and some can change their color or pattern to match different surroundings. Fish that swim at the surface often have white bellies, silvery sides, and dark-blue backs. This makes it difficult for **prey** and **predators** to spot them. When seen from above, the darker shade blends in with the sea, and when seen from below, the pale color blends with the light from the sky.
- All fish are "cold blooded." This means their body temperature is about the same as the water around them. Unlike **mammals,** such as humans, they do not make their own body heat. Like **reptiles** and **amphibians,** they depend on their **environment** to keep them at the right temperature.

Big fish

The largest fish is the whale shark, which is almost 1,500 times bigger than the goby. Some whale sharks are the size of a bus and reach 46 ft (14 m) in length. They can weigh up to 13.2 tons (12 metric tons). The next biggest fish is the basking shark, at about 40 ft (12 m) long. These fish do not attack humans.

▼ A diver is safe near the mouth of the whale shark.

predator animal that hunts and eats other animals
streamlined torpedo-shaped

Protected

A coelacanth can be the same size and weight as a human. Very little is known about this very rare fish, which is now protected by law. It lives in undersea caves 650–2,300 ft (200–700 m) deep, and it seems to be active only at night.

Bony and baffling

Fossils of bony skeletons show that an **ancient** type of fish was around long before the dinosaurs. Scientists thought this fish had been **extinct** for millions of years. Then came a great find of the 20th century. In 1938 the fish appeared alive and well in the Indian Ocean near Africa. It is called a coelacanth ("see-la-kanth"). Scientists think this **species** has remained unchanged for 400 million years, even though each fish only lives for up to 60 years.

Others have been found since. A scientist from California was on vacation in Indonesia in 1997. In the middle of a fish market, he saw a strange blue fish on one of the slabs. His mouth dropped open when he realized it was a coelacanth. Another one had been found.

▼ The rare coelacanth was a great discovery of the last 100 years.

ancient   from a past age long ago
extinct   has died out, never to return

Top of the range

The marlin is related to the swordfish family. The swordfish's sharp bony jaw has been known to **pierce** wooden boats. Another super-fast member of the family is the sailfish (shown below). This has a large fin that sticks up like a huge sail on a boat.

▲ A marlin leaps from the sea with a remora fish hitching a fast ride.

Fastest

The blue marlin is sometimes called the sea-cheetah because it is such a fast hunter. It is built for speed with its super-**streamlined** shape. Its fins can fold away into grooves in its body to reduce any **friction**. This allows it to reach speeds of 50 mi (80 km) per hour. The black marlin can be even faster and sometimes reaches 80 mi (128 km) per hour. Its tough backbone and skeleton give its long tail extra power.

Marlin have long pointed noses like spears. They use them to slash through tuna. They tend to hunt alone in the open ocean. A marlin can grow to be 13 ft (4 m) long and can live for about twenty years.

fossil   very old remains of things that once lived, found in mud and rock
pierce   stab or break through a surface

Bendable and big

You might think fish with soft, light, and bendable skeletons cannot be very strong. Think again. Some of these fish are the biggest and toughest of all.

Rays

Of all the **cartilaginous** fish, the rays are the most gentle and graceful as well as the strongest. There are around 450 types of ray. They all "fly" and glide gracefully along the seabed. Their wide fins flap slowly like a bird's wings. Some rays can grow to be over 13 ft (4 m) across.

Most rays feed on shellfish and worms that they uncover on the seabed. When they need to hide, they lie still and cover themselves with sand. Manta rays often sweep up to the surface. At times they leap out of the water in a somersault.

Secrets of the bat ray

This ray is dark brown with a white belly and large eyes. Its two long fins look like a bat's ears. Its flat body has a long, whiplike tail armed with a stinger. If stepped on or attacked, stingrays can inject poison from their tail spines to kill their attacker. They may swim alone or in groups, as shown above.

prey   animal that is killed and eaten by other animals

Sharks

There are nearly 400 types of shark. All but a couple live in the sea. They do not have scales like other fish. In fact, their rough skin is covered with tiny pointed "teeth." If you stroke a shark the wrong way, it can even cut your skin.

Very few sharks are dangerous. Some are even gentle and shy. One of these is the hammerhead shark. It is called this because of the strange shape of its flat head, with eyes at each end. In fact, its head has thousands of tiny **receptors** along the edges. One is a scent **sensor** that tells the shark when **prey** is near. A direction sensor tells it how far away the prey is.

Hammerheads

These sharks can grow to be 13 ft (4 m) long, but they very rarely attack humans. As with all sharks, they are in greater danger from us than we are from them. Hammerheads like the one on the left are caught mainly for the oil in their livers, which is rich in vitamin A. They feed on smaller sharks and fish buried in sand.

◄ Manta rays often rise to the surface of the ocean.

receptor   organ in the body that responds to a signal
sensor   device that detects and measures a type of signal

Amazing Bodies

Gills

Gills are feathery structures on the sides of a fish's head. Water comes in its mouth and passes out through the gill slits. The gills of a healthy fish are bright red because of the high level of oxygen in the many **blood vessels.** Without oxygen, the gills would be brown.

The big question that puzzled people for centuries was: "How do fish breathe?" If all life on our planet needs **oxygen** to **survive,** how do animals breathe where there is no air? The answer is that fish do not need air, but they do need oxygen. There is plenty of oxygen in seas and rivers. At least, there should be.

Breathing

Just as we send air in and out of our nose and mouth all the time, fish keep gulping in water to pass out through their gills. Just like our lungs, the fish's gills take in oxygen and pass out **carbon dioxide.** And just like us, fish can "drown" if they do not get the right mix of oxygen into their blood.

▲ These gills of an Atlantic salmon are healthy and red.

► Polluted water stops fish from breathing, so they soon die.

Wild Words   blood vessel   fine tube that carries blood all around the body
carbon dioxide   gas that animals and humans breathe out

When fish cannot breathe

When small ponds dry up, all the fish crowd into the water that is left. If they use up all the oxygen in the water, they "drown." Fish can also drown if their gills are hurt in a fight.

If the oxygen supply in the water is getting very low, fish will rise to the surface. Bony fish can suck air at the surface into a saclike **organ** called an air bladder. Some fish take oxygen out of this air instead of straight from the water. But when the surface of the water freezes in winter, the fish cannot reach that air and they may die.

Plants in water make oxygen. If **pollution** kills the plants, it will also kill the fish, since there will not be enough oxygen for them to breathe.

News flash: Herbert the Turbot!

This story shows how some fish can survive for hours without breathing:

Michael Reeves caught a 2.2-lb (1-kg) turbot in Dorset, England, in 2002. He took it home and put in the fridge. Fifteen hours later, the fish moved, so he rushed it to a local **aquarium**. The cold fridge had slowed the fish down and kept it living. Today Herbert swims happily on, alive and well.

pollution   ruining natural things with dangerous chemicals, fumes, or garbage
survive   stay alive despite danger and difficulties

Lungfish

Every family has its odd member. Fish have a very odd family member. The lungfish goes against all the rules of fish breathing—it has lungs as well as gills. This means it can behave strangely.

There are actually six **species** of lungfish known today. All six can breathe air when they need to. In addition to using gills when they are swimming underwater, they can go up to the surface and gulp down air. It means lungfish can leave the water and live on land.

These fish look like eels and live in lakes or rivers in Australia, South America, and Africa. The South American lungfish can grow to more than 3 ft (1 m) long. The African lungfish can reach more than 6.5 ft (2 m) in length.

Beware of lungfish

Even though lungfish can breathe air, it would not be smart to lift one out of the water. It would not harm the fish to be picked up, but it could be risky for the person. Lungfish will attack almost anything that moves, including human hands.

▲ It is best to keep lungfish in their own tank, since they are fearless and will attack anything.

slither   slip and slide along like a snake

Survival

The African lungfish has two lungs, which it uses when ponds dry up in the dry season. It buries itself in the mud and curls up. It makes extra slime that hardens to make a crust. The lungfish can then live through the dry season until the rain comes. When it gets wet outside again, the lungfish wakes up and **slithers** off to look for a pond. Scientists have even kept lungfish out of water for four years.

The Queensland lungfish of Australia has one lung. When its stream dries up, it pokes its head above the water to fill the lung. The sound it makes is said to be like a **wheeze.** This lungfish can only **survive** a few days out of water.

Lungfish supper

Some people in Africa like to eat lungfish. How do people find them when they are buried deep in mud? They pretend to be rain by tapping their fingers on the ground. The lungfish "wake up" and think it is time to head for water.

▲ An African lungfish crawls across dry land.

wheeze   whistling, chesty sound made when breathing

Living on land and water

Eels can be something of a mystery. There are nearly 700 different kinds. Some of them seem to look more like snakes or **amphibians** than fish. Yet they are fish—and most live on the seabed.

The eels that live in some lakes, ditches, and rivers do strange things. Some nights, they are on the move. They leave their fish world and become creatures of the land. They take **oxygen** from the air instead of from water. Just like amphibians, they can breathe through their skin without needing lungs. For years, people used to wonder how a new pond, miles from anywhere, suddenly became so full of eels. Where did they come from? The answer is simple. The eels **slithered** miles by themselves, breathing fresh air.

Land fish

Eels survive in almost any type of water, including salt, fresh, still, or flowing. They live at the bottom of the water, under stones, and in mud. Those that travel over land eat worms, insects, or maybe a frog as they go.

▶ A European eel leaves its river to explore the land.

amphibian   cold-blooded animal that lives in water or on land
Everglades   large area of swamp in Florida

Common eel

The common eel can live out of water as long as it keeps cool and damp. By breathing through its skin, it takes in about half the amount of oxygen it would get from using its gills in water.

Asian swamp eel

The Asian swamp eel is more of a problem because it **survives** very well out of water. In the 1990s these eels somehow arrived in Florida. Ever since, they have been slithering across the **Everglades,** eating many small animals on their way. At 3.3 ft (1 m) long, the swamp eel hides in swamps, ponds, canals, roadside ditches, and rice fields. If the water dries up, it just slithers into mud or grass and lives there for months with no food.

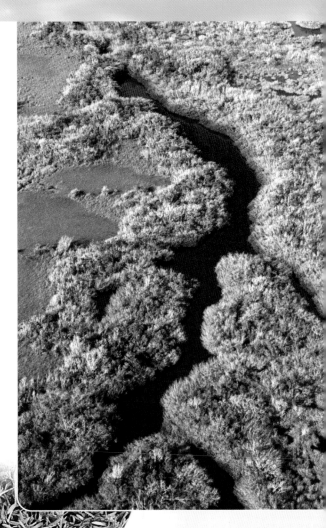

Pests

Scientists have tried all sorts of ways to control the swamp eels in the Florida Everglades, shown above. Nothing really works. Poison does not affect them. Draining ponds is useless, since they would slither away somewhere else. Even explosives do not seem to harm them. They are tough fish!

oxygen one of the gases in air and water that all living things need

Feeding

Cleaning up the sea floor

Cod feed by sucking up food on the seabed. In 2000 some Australian fishermen caught a cod that was about 5 ft (1.5 m) long and cut it open. A man's head was in its stomach! Police believe that the man fell into the sea, and then scavenging fish ate the body.

▼ A diver meets a potato cod at the Great Barrier Reef, Australia.

When it comes to feeding, there are four main types of fish.

- **Grazers,** or plant-eaters, such as parrot fish or grass carp.
- **Scavengers,** which eat any waste matter on the seabed, including meat killed by other fish. Cod suck up all kinds of food in this way.
- Meat- and insect-eaters, which kill their own food, such as mackerel.
- **Sifters,** which eat tiny particles, such as basking sharks.

Grazing

Plant-eaters tend to graze in shallow coastal waters where there is **algae** on the sea floor. They learn to scrape algae and sea urchins off rocks or to nibble at seaweed.

Scavengers

The **sediment** on the ocean floor contains a lot of food. Scraps fall to the seabed, and many fish simply pick up the pieces. They are the cleaners of the oceans.

algae   type of simple plant without stems that floats or grows in water or on rocks

Killers

Predators that kill other fish have to track down and chase their **prey**. Some patiently wait to attack their food. Fish such as tuna travel long distances to search for food. Once they have found smaller fish, they need sharp teeth to eat them. **Carnivorous** fish have developed strong mouths to catch prey and swallow it whole or in large pieces.

Sifters

Filter feeders are fish that **sieve** food from water. Water is full of tiny particles of food. The fish suck in water and sift out the bits of food, such as very tiny animals or plant bits. Even some large sharks, such as whale sharks, feed like this. Although whales are **mammals,** many of them are also filter feeders. They eat very tiny animals called **krill.**

Can fish taste their food?

Even though fish gulp pieces of food down whole, they do have taste buds in and around the mouth. Fish such as catfish (above) have taste buds on their **barbels.** These are like whiskers around their mouths. They are used to find food.

◄ Grazing damsel fish pick algae from coral.

carnivorous   animal that eats other animals
sediment   matter that sinks to the bottom of the sea

Fish that bite

Some fish bite anything that looks like a passing meal. Sometimes it may be a human. One of the largest freshwater fish is the giant catfish. Some have been said to reach 9.8 ft (3 m) long and weigh up to 550 lb (250 kg). Stories tell of small dogs and ducks swimming happily until a giant catfish strikes. It will often swallow **prey** whole, since it does not have sharp teeth for tearing. Because of this, some people fish for giant catfish by putting their hand down into a dark hole. They let the fish swallow their arm and then scoop it out. Sometimes people have drowned by finding such a fish far too big to handle.

▲ Catfish may sense when they are in danger of being caught.

Pike

Some pike can grow to 5 ft (1.5 m). They live in rivers and eat fish, birds, and small mammals—and sometimes people's fingers or toes. A Russian fisherman caught one and kissed it on the mouth. The fish bit his nose and would not let go, even when friends cut off the pike's head. The pike's head had to be removed at the hospital.

▶ The snakefish is long enough to coil itself around. It is sometimes known as a ropefish.

mammal   warm-blood animal with hair that feeds its young with milk

Snakefish

The snakefish is like an eel, with a large mouth and sharp teeth. Some grow to more than 3 ft (1 m) long. They eat fish, frogs, birds, and small **mammals.** They hit the news in the United States in 2002.

Another sighting of snakefish in the U.S.

Snakefish come from Asia and Africa, but they have appeared in Crofton Pond, Maryland.

It seems a number were brought into the United States and let loose. The fish are described as looking like "something from a bad horror movie."

This **predator** fish can crawl over land and live out of water for a few days. It is thought they are also **breeding** in Lake Wylie in North Carolina. If so, they could soon empty the lake of all its other fish.

Stitches needed for tiger muskie victims

The largest pike (shown below) live in freshwater in North America. These muskies can weigh 66 lb (30 kg). A 3.3-ft- (1-m-) long tiger muskie took a bite from a fourteen-year-old boy's wrist in 1995. He had been swimming in Lake Rebecca, Minnesota. A similar muskie bit a chunk from a boy's foot in Twin Valley Lake, Wisconsin, in 1998. He needed 60 stitches. So beware of muskies!

Piranha fact file

- There are over 20 different types of piranha fish.

- Only four types of piranha are thought to be of danger to humans.

- Some piranhas are **vegetarian.**

- Other piranhas are **cannibals** and will eat their own young.

Man-eaters of the river

Piranha fish have a bad name for killing people. In fact, these small fish are not always as deadly as some stories suggest. The name *piranha* means "tooth fish," or "scissors." That is because some do have little razor-sharp teeth. But they do not always attack. They can be very nonthreatening.

Red-bellied piranhas are the more fearsome fish in this family. They can grow up to 14.2 in. (36 cm) long and can give quite a bite. They tend to swim in groups called a **shoal.** At times they become aggressive and look out for **prey** to attack. In the dry season, the rivers lose water and the fish get hungry. They soon sense any blood in the water. That is when they seem to go crazy in a feeding **frenzy.**

▶ A shoal of piranha can soon kill a sick animal struggling in the water.

cannibal   animal that eats its own species
frenzy   wild fury or excitement

Eaten alive!

A few stories tell of people or animals falling into a river that quickly bubbles with thrashing piranhas. The fish strip the flesh from their **victim** in a matter of minutes. Such stories are rare and happen mostly in horror movies. Even so, people who fish in rivers of South America have to be careful. Many have lost toes or fingers when they waded in the water. Red-bellied piranhas do an important job. They help to get rid of sick or weak animals that fall into the water. They clean up the river and can even stop disease from spreading.

Bigger man-eater

Bull sharks like the one below can live in the sea and in rivers. They have been known to swim for miles up rivers in South Africa. Some have even attacked small boats. These 9.8-ft- (3-m-) long sharks are known for killing a few people each year. They are also called Zambezi sharks.

shoal group of fish; sometimes called a school
vegetarian animal that does not eat meat; sometimes called a herbivore

The biggest

The biggest great white shark to be caught was a female. It was 21 ft (6.4 m) long and was caught in 1945 in the sea off Cuba. It weighed 7,300 lb (3,312 kg) and was 14.8 ft (4.5 m) around its middle.

Man-eaters of the sea

There may be around 100 attacks on people each year from all types of sharks. Less than half of these attacks will kill someone. Yet people kill about 100 million sharks each year. This can be for sport, for food, or just to keep beaches "shark free" for tourists.

Great white sharks

The great white shark attacks more people than any other shark. Great whites simply bite things to see if they are worth eating. Sometimes they bite surfers who look like seals from below. The attacks are usually reported about on television. News reports and movies such as *Jaws* make us think the great white shark is the all-time big bad fish.

◄ Sharks lose and grow their teeth throughout their life.

fatal   causing death

Tiger sharks

The next shark the world loves to hate is the tiger shark. Again, this shark attacks just a few people each year. It is usually 10–13 ft (3–4 m) long, but some have reached more than 22 ft (7 m). The tiger shark has a blunt snout and stripes on its back. It lives in warm seas around the world and tends to swim near the surface. It can reach speeds of 20 mi (32 km) per hour and can travel up to 50 mi (80 km) a day.

Tiger sharks rely on their keen sense of smell to detect **prey**. They will eat almost anything, including seals, turtles, seabirds, fish, sea snakes, other sharks, and garbage. Fishermen have found all sorts of things inside tiger sharks, such as bottles, cans, license plates, tires, ships' anchors . . . and bits of humans!

Great barracuda

They call the barracuda (shown above) "the tiger of the sea," since it is a fierce hunter in the Caribbean. It can reach 6 ft (1.8 m) in length and weigh 88 lb (40 kg). It also has savage teeth. Although not really man-eaters, giant barracudas have given humans nasty wounds. These are not **fatal**, but they usually need stitches.

◀ The stripes give tiger sharks their name.

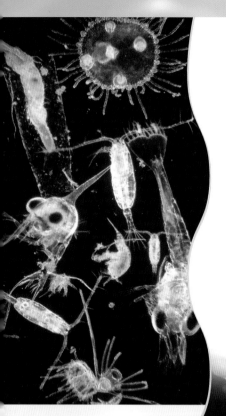

Gentle giants

As the biggest known fish in the world, the whale shark can look scary. In fact, these large sharks have a gaping mouth because they are feeding all the time. They need to, because they weigh as much as six elephants. They have huge mouths up to 4.6 ft (1.4 m) wide. Their skin can be 4 in. (10 cm) thick, the thickest skin of any living animal. They live in deep, warm seas and often **cruise** near the surface.

Whale sharks are filter feeders. They swim slowly, sucking up water full of **plankton** and tiny fish. They pump the filtered water out through their gills. Whale sharks usually stay on their own and just meet in groups now and then. They swim gently and are harmless to humans.

Plankton: The sea's life-line

Plankton forms the base of the **food chain** in the ocean. Many **species** feed on this "soup" of tiny particles that float in the sea. Plankton is made up of **microscopic** plants and animals and tiny eggs of crabs or fish such as herring. The picture above shows plankton highly magnified.

▲ The huge whale shark feeds only on tiny plankton.

cruise   travel gently, with no rush
food chain   order in which one living thing feeds on another

Krill

Krill are one of the most important food sources in the ocean. They are tiny shrimplike animals that drift in the sea. Filter feeders eat many tons of this **protein**-rich food every day. Scientists think that all the krill in the ocean (716.5 million tons) would weigh more than all the humans on Earth.

Basking sharks

Basking sharks are the next biggest fish in the world. Some weigh about 4.4 tons (4 metric tons). The largest recorded basking shark was 40.4 ft (12.3 m) long. On average, females are about 29.5 ft (9 m) and males are nearly 23 ft (7 m) long. They live in the Atlantic and Pacific oceans and are seen off European coasts.

Like whale sharks, basking sharks drift slowly through the sea with their huge mouths filtering out plankton. They may take in about 396,000 gallons (1.5 million liters) of water an hour. Five thousand slits in their gills strain the food. In winter, they lose these, so they cannot feed during this time. These huge sharks sometimes gather in large groups of 100 or more. When young are born, they are 5 ft (1.5 m) long.

plankton tiny plants, eggs, and animals that drift in the sea
protein nutrient in food that is used by the body for growth and repair

Breeding

Like all animals, fish have a strong **instinct** to increase the number of their **species**. They spend a lot of energy finding a mate to create and raise young fish.

Reproduction

So many things affect how often different fish breed. Light, heat, tides, and food supply are all important in **reproduction.** So is the water itself. **Pollution** not only harms eggs, it can also make fish change sex. This can mean a species may stop breeding completely.

Meeting

Fish use many tricks to attract a mate. Some perform all kinds of dancing displays, while others show off bright colors. In the deep sea, where it is dark, fish like the lantern fish light up to say, "I am yours!"

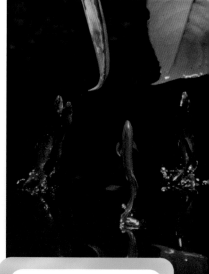

▲ Female splash tetra lay eggs on leaves. Males flick water to keep the eggs wet.

Mating

The usual way that fish **breed** is for the male to **fertilize** the female's eggs by moving beside her and releasing **sperm** as she releases her eggs. Some females, like guppies and sharks, keep the eggs inside their bodies. The young hatch inside and are born live into the water. Some fish eggs may take just one day to hatch. Others take up to many months.

► Lantern fish use lights to find each other in the dark, deep water.

fertilize   when a sperm joins an egg and makes a new individual
instinct   fixed way of behaving that comes naturally

Looking after the family

The male three-spine stickleback builds a nest out of weed to attract a female. He glues it together by a sort of cement made by his kidneys.

The female splash tetra of South America lays her eggs on leaves by leaping out of the river. The male then leaps out to fertilize them. He keeps the eggs wet by splashing them with his tail until they hatch.

Some bony fish are both sexes in one. A single fish makes both sperm and eggs. Some fish of the wrasse family are born female and later become male. Some damselfish are born as males and change into females. Sea bass can change from female to male and then back again. Being a fish can be very confusing!

Can you believe it?

The mola, or ocean sunfish, lays up to 50 million eggs at one time. Cod can lay eight million. If the eggs all **survived,** the sea would be packed with fish. Some sharks, however, only produce a few eggs at a time.

▲ These Californian sunfish produce a huge amount of eggs.

reproduction   producing more of the same species
sperm   male sex cell

Struggle

Fish ladders (shown on the right, below) are often used in rivers where salmon swim. People put them by **dams** in the rivers to help salmon get back to their spawning grounds. Each female salmon lays 2,500 to 7,000 eggs. Very few eggs will ever develop into adult fish.

Spawning salmon

The way some salmon **spawn** is one of the wonders of nature. Atlantic and Pacific salmon sense the right time to leave the sea. They swim thousands of miles up rivers to **breed.** They head for the exact stream in the hills where they once hatched. Their journey is full of danger as they struggle upstream. Sometimes they have to leap up waterfalls and avoid **predators** such as bears and eagles.

Those salmon that make it "home" dig a nest in the gravel. The female lays her eggs and the male **fertilizes** them. By now, the starved Pacific salmon are so worn out that they soon die. Their eggs must **survive** without them.

abdomen   middle part of the body around the stomach
breed   produce offspring

New life

The newly hatched young salmon stay buried in the gravel nest. They feed on stores of **nutrients** from egg yolks attached to their **abdomens.** When the yolks are gone, the young salmon leave the nest. They now begin to eat tiny plants and insects.

Soon the small fish begin their long journey downstream to the sea. Many will not survive because other fish will eat them. Those salmon that make it to the sea will live there and grow for up to four years. Some will reach over 3 ft (1 m) long and weigh as much as 66 lb (30 kg). At last, it is time for them to swim toward their birthplace to spawn.

The eel's story

Freshwater eels live in rivers and lakes, but they travel thousands of miles to spawn at sea. American and European eels breed in the Sargasso Sea near Florida. Years after hatching, the small eels swim up rivers to where they grow. Then it is back to sea to spawn and die.

◀ With their long journey nearly over, salmon are still not safe from hungry grizzly bears.

dam wall built to hold back water
spawn lay eggs in water and fertilize them

Did you know?

- Baby seahorses must rise to the surface to gulp air when they are born. This air fills their **swim bladder** and lets them float.

- The common seahorse of the Atlantic coast of North America grows to over 5 in. (13 cm) in length. The Pacific seahorse can grow to 12 in. (30 cm).

▶ Most young seahorses take a year to mature.

Strange parents

The most unusual fish, when it comes to producing young, must be the seahorse. The parents go against all the rules. It is the father who gives birth. The mother does not have much to do with the babies at all.

Seahorses tend to be partners for life. The female lays 100–200 eggs inside a pouch on the front of the male. She does this by dropping the eggs through a tube put into his pouch. The male lets **sperm** into his pouch, and the eggs are **fertilized.** For a few weeks, the young seahorses grow inside his pouch. He feeds them with juices made by his body.

swim bladder   air sac inside bony fish that stops them from sinking

Birth

The time comes for the male seahorse to give birth. It can take him two days, and he seems worn out afterward. His pouch begins to squeeze the young seahorses and push them out.

Clumps of young fish shoot out from his pouch. Some are only 0.4 in. (1 cm) long. As soon as they are born, the small seahorses begin to look after themselves.

Although seahorses keep their partners for life, some female seahorses may have more eggs than a male's pouch will carry. In that case, she looks for a second male to carry the rest of her eggs. If a male still has room left in his pouch for more eggs, he will mate with another female to fill his pouch.

Pipefish

Like its cousin the seahorse, the pipefish (shown above) has a long snout and no teeth. The male keeps the eggs in his pouch before he gives birth.

The largest pipefish grow to about 20 in. (50 cm) long.

◄ Baby seahorses are being born from this male seahorse's pouch.

Defense

It is not easy being a small fish. Everyone wants to eat you! Many fish have developed all kinds of ways to stay alive in a hungry world.

Kill or cure

The electric torpedo ray (shown below) gives shocks to its prey from fins near each eye. In **ancient** Roman times, doctors used to strap a live ray to a patient's head. It was meant to cure a headache!

Electric

Some fish have a special weapon: electricity. Even though this power is used to help fish find their way around, it can also come in very handy when they are under attack. A few fish make **electric fields** and use special **sensors** along their bodies. These "read" what is going on around them. It is like getting lots of quick photo images back.

Seawater **conducts** electricity better than freshwater. Fish in the sea therefore do not have to make very much electricity. Even so, a torpedo ray can give out 220 volts. That is enough to give you a real shock.

aquarium   place containing tanks of living fish
conduct   transmit energy

Live wires

Electric eels live in rivers in South America. They can shoot out over 600 volts of electricity or sometimes as much as 800 volts. That is enough to kill a horse. It could be **fatal** for a person standing on an electric eel. The fish has electric cells in its tail that slowly charge up like a big battery. This energy helps to guide the eel in murky water. And that is where it is easy to step on one. The eel uses these shock tactics to stun its **prey** and also to harm any attacker.

The stargazer fish is in the perch family. It waits in sand to stun any passing prey using electric organs between its eyes. If something tries to eat it, it must be like chewing a live wire.

High voltage

The electric catfish lives in Africa and can grow to more than 3 ft (1 m) long. It can give a quick zap of up to 350 volts of electricity to stun prey or keep **predators** away. It also seems to respond to **currents** in Earth a few hours before an earthquake strikes.

▼ Some electric eels can grow to almost 10 ft (3 m) long.

▼ An electric catfish can only share an **aquarium** with its own young. Any other fish would die of shock.

current   movement of electrical energy
electric field   area affected by electrical energy

The lionfish

The lionfish belongs to the deadly scorpion fish family. It has poisonous spines. People can get a nasty poke, but they usually **survive**, in spite of great pain. The venom in the spines remains active for days. Lionfish live on the Great Barrier Reef in Australia.

Poison

The best way small fish can stop bigger fish from eating them is to taste horrible or to be deadly. In fact, some small fish can kill people with their **venom.** One of these is the stonefish, which grows to 14 in. (35 cm). Its venom can be deadly. It lies on the seabed with spikes sticking up to stop sharks from eating it. But if a person steps on one, it can be very dangerous. These fish live in the sea off northern Australia.

Surgeonfish defend themselves by being sharp like knives. Spikes tipped with venom flick out from their tails when they are under threat. They can give people nasty cuts, but nothing worse. These fish can be 8–39.5 in. (20–100 cm) long and come from Hawaii.

▶ Lionfish are easy to see. With sharp spines like these, they don't have to worry about hiding.

antidote   medicine to make a poison safe
gene   information in living things that tells how they will grow

◀ When danger strikes, a pufferfish fills with water to defend itself.

The zebra fish

Zebra fish (shown below) from Southeast Asia have poison **glands** at the base of their fins. These fish are now of great interest to science. Zebra fish make ideal models for research into **genes**, since they have similar gene patterns to humans. Doctors are using this fish to study diseases that affect humans.

The pufferfish

The pufferfish got its name because it puffs up to about twice its normal size by gulping water when it is threatened. Pufferfish range in size from just a few inches long to almost 23.5 in. (60 cm). There are 100 different sorts that live in the Pacific and Indian oceans. When it puffs up like a ball, a pufferfish can swim at only about half its normal speed. But it does not have to hurry. Its spines stick out like a porcupine's. Nothing would try to swallow that. Even if it did, the poison inside the fish could be deadly. Some of its **organs** are full of poison. Even cooking does not make the fish safe. People have died from eating it, since there is no known **antidote**.

gland   part of the body that makes hormones and other substances
venom   poison

37

Hide and seek

One way to keep away from hungry mouths is to hide inside a safe one—mom's mouth! Some fish are called mouthbreeders because the mother protects her eggs and young by holding them in her mouth. One sign of trouble and in they all go!

Camouflage

Another way to avoid being eaten is by using **camouflage.** Many fish seem **invisible** when their colors match their backgrounds. Others have stripes that break up their shape and make them harder to see. Some fish look like stones or weeds. And others can turn to one side and almost disappear because they are flat. Such camouflage is a lifesaver.

Flatfish

Flatfish cannot swim fast, but they can squeeze into cracks to escape. They can also lie flat on the seabed—no one will know they are there. They have both eyes on one side of their body. Some, like the sculpin and flounder, can change color to match the sand. Others just cover themselves in sand and lie flat until danger has passed.

▲ In some **species** of mouthbreeder, the male may look after the young.

coral reef   ridge in warm seas made of the skeletons of millions of tiny sea animals

Moray eels

Moray eels hide in nooks and crannies in rocks. Only their eyes can be seen as they wait for a passing fish dinner. At the same time, larger fish cannot see or get at the moray in its little den. Chain morays live in the shallow reefs and rocky coastlines of the Caribbean. Their golden, chainlike patterns camouflage their movements as they **slither** around in search of crabs.

Stonefish

Lying on the seabed, the Australian stonefish has perfect camouflage and looks just like a crusty rock. It feeds on small fish and shrimp. When they swim by, the stonefish opens its mouth and gulps them down in less than a second.

Smelly camouflage

Some of the 80 species of parrot fish (above) have an interesting trick to defend themselves. They camouflage their smell at night so they can sleep safely in **coral reefs.** They cover themselves with a jellylike substance that stops their enemies from "sniffing them out" to eat them.

◀ When a plaice lies still on the seabed, no one is likely to see it.

invisible   not able to be seen

Weird and Wonderful

Fish behave in weird and wonderful ways. Some are extraordinary. They do things that other fish just would not attempt.

Fish that fly

Some fish can leave the water and seem to fly. In fact, a flying fish glides rather than flies. It leaps out of the sea with its fins folded and then spreads them like wings. As it skims over the water, its tail beats down to give it speed and to lift the fish above the surface. A single glide can take a fish 590 ft (180 m) over the sea. Flying fish use this trick when they need to make a quick escape. Sometimes it takes them into worse danger. Often flying fish fly right onto the decks of ships, where they get stranded.

Record

A flying fish **vibrates** its tail over 50 beats per second to get enough speed for take off. The flying fish's record is a distance of more than 650 ft (200 m). In a few glides, it can keep flying for more than 40 seconds.

▶ Flying fish leave a trail in the water as they skim the surface of the sea.

vibrate   quiver or move back and forth very quickly

So why do flying fish fly instead of swim? Simple: it is faster. Air gives less **friction** than water, so the flying fish can escape from dolphins, tuna, or other fast **predators** far more quickly. They simply leap across the surface of the sea.

Flying fish hit around-the-world sailors

RIO DE JANEIRO, Brazil—March 2002

Boats in the Volvo Ocean Race have braved a giant **waterspout** in the Sydney–Hobart race. They have had to cope with icebergs and storms in the Southern Ocean. But now, in the Caribbean, they have been battered by flying fish. Sailors are being hit as the 9.8-in. (25-cm) "winged wonders" leap out of the water at 40 mi (64 km) per hour. A number of sailors have been thumped in the chest and knocked over when the fish crash into them.

Danger

Some fish that leap out of the sea have caused nasty accidents. A man named Anthony Fernando was reported to have been killed by a garfish (below) off the coast of Sri Lanka in 1988. The fish, like a swordfish, leaped from the sea and speared his neck.

Dangerous friend

The remora fish helps to keep sharks clean by picking off parasites. It hitches a ride and sticks close to the shark's side, as shown below. The shark pays it back by being a **permanent** bodyguard and agreeing not to bite. The remora gets to eat the shark's leftovers, too.

Sticking together

Some fish have a special arrangement with other fish that is fine for both partners. At least 45 **species** have a deal with bigger fish: they clean the bigger fish, if the bigger fish agree not to kill them.

One of the busiest cleaners of the sea is the cleaner wrasse. In fact, it often has **clients** lining up to be cleaned. The wrasse eats all sorts of **parasites** from the gills and even the mouths of large **carnivorous** fish. The bigger fish just let the wrasse munch away—all around their deadly teeth and gums.

But another little fish has learned to copy the wrasse. It is called a "false cleaner." While the bigger fish happily lets it nibble away, the false wrasse suddenly bites a chunk from its client's fins. A dirty trick!

client   customer
permanent   lasting for a very long time

Doctor fish

Another fish likes to nibble away at the dead scales and skin of other animals. The bigger fish are happy to let the kangal fish of Turkey do its job. It is a member of the carp family, and it is very good at giving a sort of massage. In fact, it is sometimes called the doctor fish.

It can do humans a lot of good, too. These fish have helped people with skin problems. When they pick at scabs and sores, the fish can help to heal diseased skin. The patient just has to sit in a tub full of kangal fish and let them nibble. It might seem scary, but many people are certain it helps them get better.

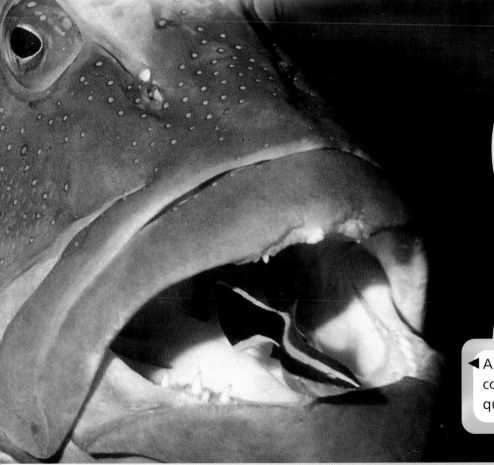

Safe

The clown fish (above) coats itself with slime. This protects it from the stinging **tentacles** of the **sea anemone** where it lives. That means other fish cannot get to the clown fish to eat it. The anemone could live without the clown fish—but not the other way round.

◀ A wrasse hops into a coral trout's mouth for a quick brush and polish!

sea anemone   sea animal that attaches itself to a rock
tentacle   body part that is like a long, thin arm

Hot and cold

The pupfish lives in hot springs in California, where the water temperature is a steaming 104 °F (40 °C). Meanwhile, the Alaska blackfish lives in ponds and streams in freezing Alaska. It can **survive** for 30 minutes in temperatures as low as –4 °F (–20 °C).

Jawless suckers

Some people go swimming in rivers and the sea and come out covered in bloodsucker fish. These fish live by feeding off others. Hagfish and lampreys are such **parasites.** They do not have jaws, but rather a mouth that sucks onto another fish. River lampreys suck out the blood and juices of any fish they can find. Sometimes three or four lampreys could be stuck on one fish. A number of different types live in rivers in the United States. Do not worry—lampreys are only small. If they suck onto a human, they can be pulled off.

A single lamprey can suck and kill as many as 40 lb (18 kg) of fish in a year. That is a big problem to the fish stocks of the Great Lakes and Chesapeake Bay.

▲ A pupfish feels at home in hot water.

indigestion   pain and difficulty in digesting food

The deep

Then there is the weird world in the deep, dark sea. Some amazing fish live miles down in the Pacific Ocean. We still do not know about many of them.

Strange anglerfish have their own "rod and line" to catch other fish. This hangs over the anglerfish's head. When the end lights up, fish are drawn to it. All the anglerfish has to do is open its mouth and eat the fish.

The hairy anglerfish is covered in spines that pick up vibrations in the water. This helps them to find **prey** in the dark. The "hairy angler" just opens its huge mouth, filled with teeth. Its stomach can swell so much that it can swallow prey larger than itself.

Moray eel facts

- **Ancient** Romans bred moray eels in seaside ponds and are thought to have fed them with live slaves who were considered bad.

- There are about 80 **species** of moray eel. Their flesh can be **toxic**. King Henry I of England (1068–1135) is believed to have died from **indigestion** caused by eating a moray eel.

◀ In deep, dark waters, prey can only see the light on the anglerfish's rod. It's just as well they can't see its face!

toxic poisonous

Fish in Danger

The Great Barrier Reef

The Great Barrier Reef, off Australia's east coast, is home to more than 1,500 species of fish; 4,000 types of mollusk; and more than 200 species of bird. At more than 1,000 miles (1,600 kilometers) long, this reef is the biggest structure ever built by living things. It can be seen clearly from space, stretched across the dark-blue sea.

Like many places on Earth, our oceans are at risk. They are changing fast.

Coral reefs

About one third of all fish **species** live in **coral reefs**. About three million animal species such as **mollusks,** jellyfish, starfish, and **crustaceans** take shelter and feed on coral reefs. Coral reefs are one of the richest **habitats** on Earth, but they only make up one percent of the oceans.

Coral is made up of the skeletons of tiny jellylike animals with **tentacles.** They are like very small **sea anemones.** Each tiny animal, called a polyp, joins with others to make forests of colored coral reefs. When they die, the coral turns white. Coral reefs are under great threat from **pollution.** It is feared that only 30 percent of today's coral reefs will remain in 50 years.

crustacean   sea animal with jointed legs and a hard shell, such as a crab
exhaustion   tired to the point of collapse

Seahorses under threat

Coral reefs are full of life and are rich in food. Some of the most colorful **shoals** of fish live on reefs. Reefs are also the home to species of brightly colored seahorses. Seahorses fix themselves to the coral with their tails and wait for shrimp to swim by. To catch them, the seahorse just straightens its tail and rises up. The small fins on its back push it through the water. But rough waves can tear seahorses off the coral, and they soon die of **exhaustion.**

Humans are the biggest threat to the coral's seahorses. Twenty million seahorses are harvested each year for making traditional medicines. The world seahorse population has dropped by 50 percent in the last 10 years. These amazing animals are now at great risk.

Color under the sea

The warm, light, shallow water where corals grow is just right for **algae.** Algae grows on the coral and helps it to harden. Many species feed off the algae, like the brightly colored mandarin fish shown above. Fish in the coral reefs are full of color.

◄ Coral reefs support a mass of colorful fish of all sizes. Some divers say the moving shoals of fish look like liquid rainbows.

habitat   natural home of an animal
mollusk   soft-bodied animal without a backbone and often with a shell

Threat

The southern bluefin tuna is one of the largest bony fish in the world at more than 13 ft (4 m) long. It has been so heavily fished that it is nearly extinct. The flesh has a high fat content and is prized in Japan. One large fish weighing up to 2,000 lb (900 kg) can fetch over $10,000.

Endangered fish

The spotted handfish is one of the world's most **endangered** sea fish. This pear-shaped fish has fins like hands that allow it to "walk" along the sea floor. It is cream in color with yellow-brown spots. The pattern on each fish is **unique**—just like fingerprints. Like the anglerfish, the spotted handfish has a small **lure** just above its mouth. But it does not seem to use this to attract prey, so the purpose is a mystery.

Spotted handfish were common in Tasmania until the 1980s. Just two were seen between 1990 and 1994. By 2001 there were only three **breeding** groups. The arrival of the Northern Pacific seastar fish into this area may be the problem. The seastar is a **predator** and eats the handfish's eggs.

endangered   at risk of disappearing forever
lure   thing used to attract—for example, bait used to catch a fish

Sturgeon

The Baltic sturgeon can reach 11.5 ft (3.5 m) in length, but it is not the fish itself that people want to eat when they catch it. The sturgeon's eggs are used to make caviar. The United States is the world's biggest caviar importer. People can pay $100 for just 1.8 oz (50 g). Sturgeon can lay millions of sticky eggs at one time, but they have now been fished until they are almost **extinct**. So many eggs are taken to make caviar that now very few fish are hatching. Today it is a **protected species.**

The largest sturgeon in the world is the Beluga. It grows to 16.4 ft (5 m) in length and is the rarest sturgeon of all. It is the most expensive fish in the world, but there are now hardly any left in Russia's Caspian Sea.

Very rare

In just one river cave in Namibia, Africa, there are a few very rare catfish. These cave catfish (shown below) lack color because their world is so dark. They are a pale pinkish white and look kind of like an eel. Their eyes are either very tiny or covered with skin. If the water level drops in the cave, the species could disappear forever.

◀ The spotted handfish is now so rare it is a protected species.

protected species   animals that it is against the law to harm or kill
unique   there is only one of its kind

Overfishing

Bluefin tuna are one of the most valuable fish in the sea. Eighty-eight thousand tons (80,000 metric tons) were caught every year in the early 1960s. The number of adult bluefins in the western Atlantic is thought to have dropped almost 90 percent since 1970. They may not survive long into the 21st century.

Save our seas

There is no doubt that many fish are under great threat today. Our rivers and oceans are in more danger now than at any time. Over 97 percent of all life on Earth lives in the oceans, which affect the health and **survival** of all living things. But one of the biggest problems today is overfishing. Fish give humans the greatest supply of the world's **protein,** but too much is being taken out of the sea. Many fish are caught before they are old enough to **breed,** so no young are replacing them. We take out tons of fish each day and replace them with tons of garbage. We are slowly poisoning our seas.

► Oil slicks from tankers endanger life in and on the oceans.

global warming   warming up of Earth due to burning fossil fuels such as coal and oil

Sea dangers

Stocks of Atlantic cod and haddock are now very low. Bluefin tuna has also been overfished around the world. In the next few years, we are in danger of losing some **species** of fish forever unless we are more careful. **Pollution** from oil spills and chemicals from the land poison the water where fish breed.

Drilling for oil, **whaling,** and using fishing nets that tangle up too many species are putting all fish in danger. **Global warming** and dumping of waste in the sea are killing off the **coral reefs.** So we need to act now to save our oceans and the fantastic fish that share our planet in their incredible underwater world.

What can we do?

- Take an interest in what is going on in our oceans. Find out which organizations are at work and what they are doing nearest to you.

- See how organizations working to save the oceans suggest you get involved.

- Think "green" by saving energy, cutting down waste, and recycling. It all makes for a healthier planet.

whaling   hunting and killing of whales

Find Out More

Books

Sharth, Sharon. *Rays and Sharks: Underwater Predators.* Danbury, Conn.: Franklin Watts, 2002.

Sieswerda, Paul L. *Sharks. Tarrytown, NY*: Marshall Cavendish, 2001.

Silverstein, Alvin et al. *Fabulous Fish.* Brookfield, Conn.: Millbrook Press, 2003.

Spilsbury, Richard and Louise Spilsbury. *From Egg to Adult: The Life Cycle of Fish.* Chicago: Heinemann Library, 2003.

Website

Smithsonian Institute National Zoological Park
Website with articles, information, and many photos of all kinds of animals.
nationalzoo.si.edu

World Wide Web

If you want to find out more about fish, you can search the Internet using keywords such as these:

- fish
- amazing + fish
- pufferfish

You can also find your own keywords by using headings or words from this book. Use the following search tips to help you find the most useful websites.

Search tips

There are billions of pages on the Internet, so it can be difficult to find exactly what you want to find. For example, if you just type in "water" on a search engine such as Google, you will get a list of millions of webpages. These search skills will help you find useful websites more quickly:

- Use simple keywords instead of whole sentences.
- Use two to six keywords in a search, putting the most important words first.
- Be precise—only use names of people, places, or things.
- If you want to find words that go together, put quote marks around them.
- Use the advanced section of your search engine.
- Use the "+" sign between keywords to link them.

Where to search

Search engine

A search engine looks through a small proportion of the entire Web and lists all sites that match the words in the search box. It can give thousands of links, but the best matches are at the top of the list, on the first page. Try google.com.

Search directory

A search directory is like a library of websites that have been sorted by a person instead of a computer. You can search by keyword or subject and browse through the different sites like you look through books on a library shelf. A good example is yahooligans.com.

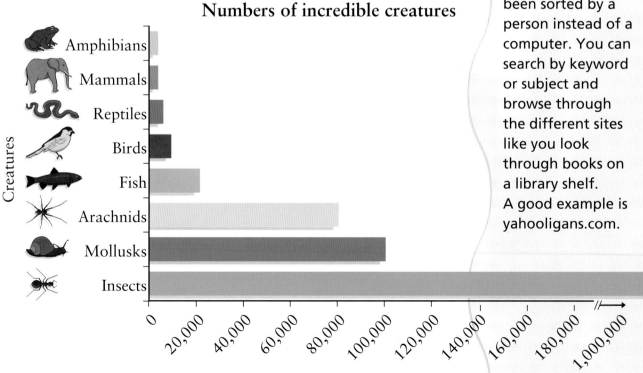

Numbers of incredible creatures

Creatures: Amphibians, Mammals, Reptiles, Birds, Fish, Arachnids, Mollusks, Insects

Number of species (approximate): 0, 20,000, 40,000, 60,000, 80,000, 100,000, 120,000, 140,000, 160,000, 180,000, 1,000,000

Glossary

abdomen   middle part of the body around the stomach

algae   type of simple plant without stems that floats or grows in water or on rocks

amphibian   cold-blooded animal that lives in water or on land

ancient   from a past age long ago

antidote   medicine to make a poison safe

aquarium   place containing tanks of living fish

barbels   body parts like long whiskers that grow from the mouths of some fish

blood vessel   fine tube that carries blood all around the body

breed   produce offspring

camouflage   color or pattern that matches the background

cannibal   animal that eats its own species

carbon dioxide   gas that animals breathe out

carnivorous   animal that eats other animals

cartilaginous   having soft, bendable gristle (cartilage) rather than bone

client   customer

conduct   transmit energy

coral reef   ridge in warm seas made of the skeletons of millions of tiny sea animals

cruise   travel gently, with no rush

crustacean   sea animal with jointed legs and a hard shell, such as a crab, shrimp, or lobster

current   movement of electrical energy

dam   wall built to hold back water

electric field   area affected by electrical energy

endangered   at risk of disappearing forever

environment   natural surroundings or habitat

Everglades   large area of swamp in Florida

exhaustion   tired to the point of collapse

extinct   has died out, never to return

fatal   causing death

fertilize   when a sperm joins an egg and makes a new individual

food chain   order in which one living thing feeds on another

fossil   very old remains of things that once lived, found in mud and rock

frenzy   wild fury or excitement

friction   drag or force when things rub together

gene   information in living things that tells how they will grow

gland   part of the body that makes hormones and other substances

global warming   warming up of Earth due to burning fossil fuels such as coal and oil

grazer   any animal that feeds only on plants such as grass or sea grass

habitat   natural home of an animal

indigestion   pain and difficulty in digesting food

instinct   fixed way of behaving that comes naturally

invisible   not able to be seen

krill   tiny shrimplike animals that swim in large numbers in the sea

lure   thing used to attract—for example, bait used to catch a fish

mammal   warm-blooded animal with hair that feeds its young with milk

microscopic   can only be seen using an instrument that magnifies tiny objects

mollusk   soft-bodied animal without a backbone and often with a shell

nutrient   important substance found in food and needed by the body

organ   part of the body that performs a particular job

oxygen   one of the gases in air and water that all living things need

parasite   animal or plant that lives in or on another living thing

permanent   lasting for a very long time

pierce   stab or break through a surface

plankton   tiny plants, eggs, and animals that drift in the sea

pollution   ruining natural things with dangerous chemicals, fumes, or garbage

predator   animal that hunts and eats other animals

prey   animal that is killed and eaten by other animals

propel   drive or push forward

protected species   animals that it is against the law to harm or kill

protein   nutrient in food that is used by the body for growth and repair

receptor   organ in the body that responds to a signal

reproduction   producing more of the same species

reptile   group of cold-blooded animals with scales, such as snakes and lizards

scavenger   animal that feeds off scraps and the prey of others

sea anemone   sea animal that attaches itself to a rock

sediment   matter that sinks to the bottom of the sea

sensor   device that detects and measures a type of signal

shoal   group of fish; sometimes called a school

sieve   sift out solids from a liquid

sifter   fish that sucks in water and filters out all the small bits of food

slither   slip and slide along like a snake

spawn   lay eggs in water and fertilize them

species   type of living animal or plant

sperm   male sex cell

streamlined   torpedo-shaped

survive   stay alive despite danger and difficulties

swim bladder   air sac inside bony fish that stops them from sinking

tentacle   body part that is like a long, thin arm

toxic   poisonous

unique   there is only one of its kind

vegetarian   animal that does not eat meat; sometimes called a herbivore

venom   poison

vertebrate   any animal that has a skeleton with a backbone

vibrate   quiver or move back and forth very quickly

victim   animal that gets hurt or killed

waterspout   twisting column of water and spray that is like a whirlwind over the sea

whaling   hunting and killing of whales

wheeze   whistling, chesty sound made when breathing

Index